The Power of Twin Soul Love

MARY DUNLOP

Copyright © 2014 Mary Dunlop

ISBN: 1493736485
ISBN 13: 9781493736485

To Mike and Mom

And when one of them meets the other half, the actual half of himself[...]the pair are lost in an amazement of love and friendship and intimacy and one will not be out of the other's sight, as I may say, even for a moment.
—Plato

Chapter 1

My grandmother was a great believer in divine connection. She had called this the purest and most authentic form of love—God's love, sewn in our soul—and her concept of it was exactly like that of the great philosopher Plato.

My grandmother, also like Plato, would refer to a soul mate as a twin. "We all have one," she'd say, "whether we realize it or not." She was a sage, my grandmother—an impassioned mystic who had me convinced in my early years that my twin kissed my soul right before I was born. Apparently, I had been born smiling, and my grandmother took this to mean that he would find me one day, that we had made a promise, and that the two of us would live happily ever after.

"Where is he, Nana?" I asked when I was almost ten years old. My brother, Johnny, who was a year younger than I, was also with us.

"You will meet him when you're ready—when your heart is ready," she assured me. For the longest time, that night remained the happiest of my life. We sat outside on our porch in southern Alberta, dreaming and watching the wind flow freely through the grass. *That's how you can see the wind*, I thought. *You can see it in trees and water. And you can see it in the way it makes grass look like silk.* My brother gently rocked in an old wooden chair that had probably come with the porch. He also wanted to know about his twin, and, with bright blue eyes peering through black lensless specs, he eagerly waited for Nana to inform him. Johnny thought the dark frames made him look like a writer, which was something he always wanted to be. He had an avid imagination, and our grandmother knew this well. "Don't worry," she said. "True love will find you, too. And with it will come great peace." She then put one arm around his shoulder and extended the other toward the sky. "Look there," she whispered. "Look at that, and I'm not just talking about the stars. Even more important are the infinite spaces in between the stars. These are the spaces God fills. Not everything can be seen. Yet, it is there. Never doubt it, and if ever you do, go outside, take a long deep breath, gaze at the stars, and then look at the spaces. Look in between. Miracles dwell in the unseen."

My grandmother, who again, like Plato, was Greek, spoke English with a hint of an accent that made her sound all the more magical, as she slowly transported us through a story of dreams. Her words were a love song written especially for us. She believed in the magic of love, and with all her heart, she wished it for my brother and me. "They are with you even now, she said. "Again, even if you can't see them, know that their love is with you all the time."

I will never forget that feeling of excitement, sheer anticipation of knowing the one—my one—was somewhere in the world. My grandmother went on to tell me that my soul twin and I were very much alike. "I see him with big round eyes and an even bigger heart." She also said that the more we loved ourselves, the more our twins would be touched by this love.

"Loving yourselves, my darlings, is the same as loving them.

"Soul twins are a gift we all receive. We don't all physically meet them. Still, they are with us, and they feel us. This is why it is twice as important to be kind to yourselves and to love yourselves no matter what. So much depends upon loving yourselves, because if you don't or if you do something to hurt yourselves, your twins will feel this somehow, wherever they are, and that precious little soul," she said (now speaking specifically to me) "who is just as beautiful as you, may not be quite as strong and could get very hurt."

"Nana!" I almost cried at the thought of my soul twin hurting. It was the strangest thing.

"You feel him." She smiled. She then paused and asked us to make her a promise. "My darlings," she said, "no matter what challenges you might face, because as beautiful as it is, life has its share of tests, promise me you will never lose faith in God, in love, or in yourselves." We both happily agreed, and Nana sealed it with a kiss—one for each of us on the forehead.

Chapter 1

I made that promise to my grandmother twenty-five years ago. Though I wasn't quite ten years old, in some way I knew who I was, and I had a clear vision of how I would honor my word. Never could I have imagined how much life would change me, or that spring, the season of renewal and growth, could be as much about endings as it is beginnings. All that magic ended when my grandmother unexpectedly died that spring. But magic, it has been said, has an instinctive way of coming back. My name is Betsey Townsend. I was a daytime television actress, whose show was hastily and unceremoniously canceled last March. Another spring brought another ending; however, this time also came a new beginning. Last spring may have marked the end of my career, but incredibly, at the same time, it brought back my grandmother's magical story.

The show—"my show", which was what I always called it—wrapped up quickly. I filmed my final episode, said my goodbyes, and then went home, took a shower and stayed under the water for an unusually long time. There was a feeling I had that I couldn't quite shake. Perhaps I hoped the water would wash it away, because I felt lost and alone. I couldn't stop thinking about how my role on "my show" was all I had. I didn't have children. I never got married. Other than a brief engagement, my life mainly revolved around work. So many of my relationships and connections seemed to have dwindled. Work was to blame for some, but that wasn't true for all. Admittedly, I couldn't hold work responsible for the circumstance that had led to the death of one of my closest friendships. The memory of how that friendship ended—with Gordo Hughes, the man who had brought me to New York—haunted me.

Gordo and I had shared a tight bond that went back to high school. I pursued him then. I admired him. This wasn't in a schoolgirl crush kind of way. Rather, I admired him for his attitude. He had this never-give-up kind of confidence that ultimately earned him two of his most heartfelt dreams.

Gordo's dreams were not in any way unreasonable or unusual. The first was one many people have. He wished to pursue an education. The problem was, he wasn't a good student. Gordo was not naturally academic. However, he would always say, "If there is a will, there is also a way." And he would find it, like he did to gain entry into the University of Alberta. That particular "way in" consisted of him taking extra courses to improve his overall grade average. It took a little time, but eventually it worked. Eventually, he was accepted into the program of his choice from where he fulfilled his first dream by graduating with a bachelor's in marketing. Gordo then moved on to focusing on his second aspiration, which was to put that degree to work. Employment opportunities in his field were scarce in Edmonton. However, once again he found a way. He took whatever he could get, including odd jobs and shift work, and saved up what he needed to make a bold move to New York. Eight years earlier, I was twenty-six, unsuccessful, and unsettled. I had pretty much given up any hope of becoming an actress until Gordo Hughes's zest for dreams inspired me to think that mine could still come true. He knew he would find the right opportunity in that big city, and as it turned out, we both did. Only three months after we left home, nine months before I landed my role on the soap, he got a top advertising position at a magazine called *Reunion*.

The magazine itself was a Manhattan based publication that had been created by a young idealist, a novelist, who was convinced of man's more spiritual nature. Mark McGregor was, at the time, only twenty-four years old, but he had already written a bestselling book on how to attract true love. *Reunion* was based on that book and quickly became as popular. Columns and articles, offering spiritual advice, appealed to adults of all ages, and the magazine's photographs of nude ethereal-like men and women captured both the eye and the imagination. Apparently, the photos were meant to reflect people's inner masculine and feminine energies, or as Gordo called it, people's inner lovers. Almost all of us have some sort of visuals or visual of our true soul mate, but rarely do we take the time to really get to know it. Gordo went on to explain that the essence of our true soul mate lies within each of us and relates to the conscious and unconscious qualities—the inner masculine and feminine energies—we each carry. For example, if a man who is in touch with his feminine qualities—his inner feminine energy— meets a woman, who does not outwardly look exactly like the perfect image of his dream girl, but inwardly she matches that energy (has the right energy, so to speak); he will still see his dream girl. That man will see his dream girl in her regardless of what she looks like on the outside. We can also take an example of a woman, a heterosexual woman, who has masculine qualities that dominate her femininity. She could, through meditation and/or imagery techniques, visualize her inner lover as a soft, nurturing feminine man and eventually realize her ideal match. In a way, this was an evolved version of Plato's theory of soul twins, which went a step further by borrowing from Jungian psychology, which sought to bring subconscious images and qualities to conscious awareness. I once read a passage in a spiritual book—one I had inherited from my grandmother—stating that the search for our ultimate partner must begin within. "Ah finally," I said to myself, after listening to Gordo. "I now know what that means."

I couldn't quite picture Gordo working for this type of magazine. I never imagined him to be a lover of spirituality or a spiritual lover. However, he went on to say, "I've always believed in this stuff. I think it's safe to assume that, at some point or another, almost everyone believes in a soul mate or twin flame."

"What about soul twin?" I asked. Gordo smiled.

People were intrigued by Mark McGregor's magazine, and among them was my brother, Johnny. He had also followed his dream. He was working as a freelance writer in Alberta, but unfortunately, opportunities for him there were as sparse as they had been for Gordo. Johnny's assignments were few and far between, so one day he asked me to have a word with Gordo about the possibility of hiring him at *Reunion*. The timing couldn't have been better. They were desperately looking for another writer. Call it kismet, call it fate—in the end, it called my brother all the way to New York.

Both Johnny and Gordo proved invaluable to *Reunion* and to their young boss whom they often found themselves defending. Mark McGregor was not a liked man in the sense that his ideas did not always conform to the cultural norm. Bloggers particularly resented him, or maybe it was just easier for them to express it. In any case, some called him cultish. Others said he was crazy—"bat-shit crazy." Most made fun of him. And many said he suffered from "magical thinking." "Guilty indeed," was what he once said in response to "magical thinking". "Why shouldn't I think magically? Magic is all around us. Life is magical!" He spoke like he wrote, in a simple honest style, and every now and then he would emphasize certain words through slightly raising his voice. I noticed this during a radio interview three years ago when he said, "Everyone, right now, gaze out your window. Take a good long look outside. Pay attention to what you're seeing and

Chapter 1

then tell me you don't agree. Isn't magic something we are ALL able to see if we try?"

I'll never forget that morning. I followed his request. I looked through my living room window and focused on a tiny pond in the park across the street. The small body of water never attracted many birds. It always seemed bleak and lonely—that was, until that moment when I looked out and saw a flock of little black birds miraculously flying around it. The beauty of their motion, the way they circled over that pond (especially because there were so many of them) left me in awe.

Mark McGregor ended his interview that day by saying, "Whether I look outside or in, I see a universe FULL of promise and opportunities." He didn't seem bat-shit crazy to me, but many continued to disagree.

My grandmother once told me to beware of throwing stones. She said that when you do, you could change a person's fate in an instant. I don't know if I ever really believed that. However, her words certainly did seem relevant to what had started happening to Mark McGregor. Three years earlier (shortly after that interview), his adversaries attacked him again, accusing him this time of making advances and taking advantage of underage girls. The allegations were unsubstantiated. McGregor called them defamation. It proved upsetting to him and to the entire *Reunion* team, but that wasn't the only misfortune to befall him. Soon after those rumors went viral, Georgia Snow, a former *Reunion* cover girl and the woman reputed to be Mark McGregor's girlfriend, was found dead at McGregor's home.

Georgia Snow had just turned twenty-six when she died. Reportedly, she had been involved in a scuffle that took place in Mark McGregor's upper-Manhattan apartment. Shortly after her death, a friend of hers, a young man she knew from her university days at NYU, said what happened didn't surprise him. The young man described Georgia, who weighed less than one hundred pounds, as being frail, "as frail in strength as she was in appearance." In a YouTube interview, he also described an incident—one that occurred years earlier at NYU—when a man accidentally bumped into her in a hallway one afternoon. Georgia's friend said, "The guy was running pretty fast; however, the force of the impact didn't seem that strong. It probably would have left most people our age stunned for a minute or two, but Georgia almost fell unconscious. I remember it as if it were yesterday. Her eyes kept opening and closing. She was making these weak whimpering sounds. I didn't know what to do, except call for help and try to keep her awake." At that point, the kind-looking young man lowered his head and re-iterated, "Georgia was not a strong girl. She would have been powerless in a rough or violent altercation." He then tearfully added that she reminded him of a bird—free-spirited and beautiful, yet delicate and weak.

Georgia's broken wrist and bruised cheek and shoulders suggested a fight violent enough to make someone of her constitution easily lose orientation or consciousness. The bruising on her cheek also indicated a powerful backhanded slap, which made investigators think that the assailant could have been male and that the attack on Georgia had been committed in a moment of passion. They didn't believe he intended to kill her. Police figured that Georgia became dizzy or lightheaded without much provocation and without her assailant taking notice. He was probably too angry or too impassioned to realize that the altercation incapacitated the young woman who helplessly fell backward and hit her head on the marble floor.

Mark McGregor's maid discovered the body. Georgia had been house-sitting for the vacationing publisher. He, at the time, was halfway around the world and therefore never considered a suspect. Or, more accurately, he was not considered one by police, because the public had been deeply influenced by those who had written against him. Bloggers had damaged McGregor's reputation almost to the point of no return. Regardless of where he was or what the police thought, people couldn't help but hold him accountable for what had happened to Georgia Snow.

Bloggers continued to write about Georgia Snow and Mark McGregor, and eventually they were joined by a local newspaper—a small time weekly publication—that ran a piece, titled "Mark McGregor—Another Kind of Predator". The paper depicted Georgia as a student, who was lured into a world she was not equipped to survive, and printed photographs of her as an adult and as a child. When words aren't enough to make people stop and think, pictures often are. Photos can be very powerful forms of influence. They can invoke both emotion and reflection, like the childhood photo of Georgia, which brought me back to remembering how full of hope I was at that age.

Chapter 1

That paper might have been small in circulation; however, reaction to its story was overwhelming—overwhelmingly negative toward Mark McGregor. He and *Reunion*'s sales took a terrible hit. My brother and Gordo were beside themselves. Johnny (now preferring to be called John) was especially angered by that story. John swiftly wrote a letter to the paper's editor, challenging her to back her article with "real data and facts." His letter went on to say that *Reunion* was a clean operation—that Mark McGregor exemplified the utmost in professional behavior—but the damage was already done. Even if the editor would have printed a retraction, it likely would have been of little help. By that time, *Reunion*'s sales were at an all-time low, and the situation got even worse when the Reverend Jeff Bay, Mark McGregor's newest adversary, entered the fray.

Reverend Bay was a feisty forty-year-old minister whose battle with *Reunion* and McGregor was inspired by moral principle. The former front man of a popular eighties boy band (if you can imagine), Jeff Bay was a handsome sympathetic, recovering alcoholic, preaching the word of God, while spending his free time helping others get sober. The guitar-toting raven-haired minister took his music to another level and quickly became a favorite of many. The reverend and his new band of young Christian fundamentalists stood hard against *Reunion* and all others like it. Reverend Bay communicated his messages through sermons, blog articles, and his live call-in Internet radio show on which he once said, "We are a people addicted." His exact words were, "Whether it be substances, money, power, electronics, or celebrity idols, we are all hooked on something, including the kind of images people like Mark McGregor feed on. I cannot stress strongly enough how much harm such people pose to our souls. God manifested in Jesus to show us the beauty of the human soul—a real beauty, not a seeming one."

My brother, by this time, was at the height of his frustration. I had never seen John so angry. In fact, I never imagined he could get that upset. "Bay's an idiot," he said, "an idiot with his own agenda. *We're* conveying the same thing. Our images are meant to reflect our spirits—the spirit and divine beauty in everyone. Jesus himself most likely did not have flowing blond or light-brown hair, fair skin, and light-colored eyes. If he did, he would have contrasted from everyone else in his region, thus contradicting what is said in the book of Matthew about Jesus looking similar to his disciples. Also, Isaiah chapter fifty-three, verse two, suggests that there was nothing particularly different or attractive about him, no beauty that we should desire him. In other words, the face of Jesus, as we have come to know it from the various Christian denominations, including Reverend Bay's, is more of an image of inner beauty than an accurate physical depiction of the man." What John said made sense; I had to agree. Maybe, if Reverend Bay would have slowed down and listened, he might have realized that he and Mark McGregor were on the same team.

Prior to Jeff Bay's vocalism, Mark McGregor was being barraged by threatening calls and letters, but there was never any fear of physical violence. He wasn't worried about his safety at all until one spooky pre-rainy night. McGregor had worked late that night and wasn't up to his usual walk home. He walked the fourteen blocks to his Upper East Side apartment in Manhattan almost every evening. However, that night, the sky looked threatening, his head hurt, and he wanted to get home quickly. He called a cab and then went outside to wait for it by the fountain. It seemed to take forever to arrive. Luckily, the fresh air felt good. Cool before the rain, it soothed his aching head and enticed him to wait a few more minutes before calling for the cab again. He also wanted to throw a coin into the fountain that towered in front of his office building. The massive structure contained hundreds of shiny wishes, and he was anxious to add one more. Just thinking about it made him smile. How could a coin ever represent something that was so priceless? Still, he searched for one. He rummaged through the left and then the right pocket of his jacket when suddenly he was interrupted by sounds of heavy footsteps and incoherent words. The noise came from behind him and rapidly got closer and louder until Mark McGregor turned to see a man, wearing a ski mask, ranting something about Jeff Bay. The man had appeared out of nowhere and violently slapped the stunned publisher across the face. The force of the blow was so strong, it caused McGregor to fall and roll down the steps that led from the fountain to the walkway. Just then, Gordo walked out of the building and was horrified to see his boss lying there with the assailant, kneeling over him, ready to strike again. Gordo panicked, as did the attacker who ran as soon as Gordo yelled.

Mark McGregor was taken to the hospital and treated for a slight concussion and broken ankle. His injuries were not deemed serious; however, emotionally the attack and ongoing stress raged on. Again, photographs are very influential. Those who had been affected by pictures of Georgia Snow were now being touched by images of a shockingly thin Mark McGregor. The public's sympathy shifted toward the gaunt young publisher, and it rose fast. People rallied around him almost as quickly as they turned their backs on Jeff Bay. "I don't pay attention to rumors," one woman said at the time, when asked for her opinion of McGregor on a public interest show called *Voice Your View*. "As far as Mark McGregor's concerned," she added, "everything alleged about him has turned out to be false. Where's the proof showing he did anything wrong? Instead of trying to destroy him, we should be admiring him. He's a gifted young philosopher, mystic, and writer. He is a lover, not a hater, and I, for one, find him inspiring." Another man, on the same show, expressed something similar by saying that anyone who wrote like Mark McGregor couldn't be anything but good.

I watched that show and breathed a sigh of relief. My brother and Gordo worked hard for that magazine; seeing it almost fall apart hurt them deeply. As for Mark McGregor, I didn't know what to make of him.

At that point, I had only met him once, shortly before he was attacked. My ex-boyfriend, Daniel, the man I was briefly engaged to, had recently popped the question, so one sunny Saturday, we dropped by my brother's for an impromptu visit to tell him the news. When we got there, John asked us to join him in the kitchen for a cup of coffee. He didn't mention he was busy, or that he had company, until I caught glimpse of a man using the phone in his study. Strangely, even then, John didn't volunteer to introduce us. He just said Mark was there to help him with an article and that he was glad we were there as he could use a break. We chatted in the kitchen for a while. Then, after half an hour or so, I excused myself and went to the study where Mark McGregor was plugging away on his laptop.

"I'm sorry," I said. "I didn't mean to scare you." His back was to the door. He hadn't heard me walk in. I gave him a bit of a jump. I think he even gasped.

"You didn't scare me," he replied. "You just surprised me a little. I'm fine."

He was a wisp of a man, thin and not very tall. His skin was almost as pale as snow, and he had uncommonly

Chapter 1

long hair that reached past his shoulders. At first glance, he wasn't much to look at, but he surprised me, too—when he smiled. He had a hauntingly beautiful smile.

Mark McGregor continued to smile while removing books and papers from the only other chair in the room. He then placed the chair beside him and invited me to sit. His eyes were hidden beneath unruly auburn bangs. I tried to catch his gaze; but for the most part, I found myself imagining what his eyes looked like by matching them to his smile and on what I could glimpse between the strands.

"Betsey," he said as soon as I sat down. His voice was warm and gentle, so gentle, it almost made feel like I was hearing my name for the first time in my life. He then asked me something peculiar. He said, "How do you know?" It was a strange question because he didn't say *what*. I had no idea what he was talking about, and instead of explaining, he reached up to rub his neck. "Mmm," he moaned. "I think I've been in front of this computer a little too long." My fiancé was still in the kitchen with my brother. Just then they shouted for me to rejoin them. Mark McGregor sighed and said, "I guess you better go."

"It's fine," I assured him. "Don't worry."

"I don't think so," he replied. "It isn't fine at all—not for me. Please leave. I'm tired, and I have a lot to do." His manner had changed so abruptly, I almost felt sick. I left the room without a word and didn't speak of him to anyone for some time. Even a short while later, when my fiancé and I parted ways, and John suggested he set me up with Mark, I simply said, "Thank you, but right now I'm not interested in dating anyone." After that, I didn't much think about Mark McGregor. I didn't really think about him at all until one night, several months later.

That night was another of those spooky dark nights that smelled of rain. I remember rushing home from the set, pouring Chardonnay into a glass, and then turning on the water to fill up my tub, before answering the phone. I wasn't going to answer it at first—I really looked forward to a long hot soak. However, the ringing was incessant. It wouldn't stop, so finally I grabbed the cordless phone off the bathroom wall and saw Gordo's name on the screen.

"Finally!" Gordo said, nervously. Apparently, he had also left messages for me on my turned-off cell. His

Chapter 1

urgency to reach me had to do with Mark McGregor. The publisher had been unwell and was staying with Gordo while waiting for his health to improve. McGregor was suffering from nausea, dizziness, and fainting spells—symptoms he attributed to the assault made upon him several weeks earlier. He was certain he had not recovered from the concussion that had left him helpless, but medical tests proved otherwise. Even though his symptoms persisted and seemed to worsen, numerous results showed nothing physically wrong with him. I listened sympathetically, as Gordo went on to tell me how badly he felt for his boss and that he didn't know how to help him. "John is here too," he said, "and neither of us knows what to do. Tonight, Mark is particularly frail and very, very frightened, which is why I'm calling you. I think seeing you might help him." I couldn't understand why he thought it would help Mark McGregor to see *me*. I still remembered his unexplainable behavior that day at my brother's. Regardless, I continued to listen. "Mark is one of your biggest fans," he proclaimed. "He watches you all the time on TV. Come on, Betsey, please. I'm not asking you for something big. It's actually very small, just a small favor, and one for which I will always be grateful." Gordo's tone was soft and kind. I should have agreed to do it. I should have done it in a second. But instead, I refused and told him I didn't think I could help. "You mean you don't want to," he responded in a voice that almost stammered. "I'm sorry," he said, "I think you just don't want to help."

Gordo hung up, rather abruptly, and I got in my bath. The rain had begun to come down. Heavy drops banged against the glass of my bathroom window. I'd never heard rain so loud. It drowned out almost every other sound—everything except the whispers of my conscience. As loud as that rain was, it wasn't loud enough to distract me from the uneasiness tugging at my chest. The bath I had longed for felt suffocating. I quickly got up and dried myself off. I had to get to Gordo's. I knew I had to. The only question now was how. A cab would have taken forever to come in that weather. A bus would have also been too slow. "If there's a will, there's a way," I almost heard him say. . . Consequently, I put on my winter/rain running shoes and ran. I ran the twenty blocks to his house.

Despite the onslaught of that rain, I got there fast, but apparently, I wasn't fast enough. When I arrived, Gordo's house was shrouded in darkness. All the lights were off. Other than a hint of movement in a curtain that almost brought one of the windows to life, everything else remained shadowed and still. Suddenly, everything felt surreal. I had a fervor to get there. I ran all that way in the rain. I was soaked from head to toe. And now, I was reluctant to ring the bell. I thought to myself I must be crazy. But what if they were sleeping?

In the end, I didn't ring the bell that night, nor did I speak to Gordo again until last May. During the third month of what I began referring to as my sabbatical, I finally mustered enough courage to call him. He had no idea of my visit to his house, and so many months had passed. I feared he'd be cold toward me or not take my call at all, but, as it turned out, my fears were wrong. Not only was he forthcoming; he was also eager to meet up.

A lot had happened since Gordo and I last spoke, including new information about the death of Georgia Snow. Police discovered several videotapes and DVDs, featuring Georgia at the hands of a simulated attacker. They all but confirmed that her death was a tragic accident. Apparently Georgia liked to play out sexual fantasies, and her favorite one was "victim." All the tapes were similar. They always featured two men. One would grab her and pretend to rough her up, while Georgia would weakly protest. She would say things like—"Stop. I'm hurt. Please, someone help me"—prompting the second man to intervene. He would then free her from the first man, and she, acting thoroughly shaken, would fake faint into his arms. It had all been done before, many times, carefully choreographed. So how did it go so terribly wrong that night? Most likely, as investigators surmised, the man attacking Georgia became a little too excited, and the rescuer was yet another who proved that being fast is not always fast enough. The tapes also confirmed that Georgia had a pre-*Reunion* drug problem when one of them—one that dated back to her university days—showed the second man carrying her unconscious body into a room where he laid her down and revived her with kisses and cocaine.

More and more details rolled in, causing the public's sympathy to flow even stronger toward Mark McGregor. Bloggers and press lost interest in him after finding a new target in the Reverend Jeff Bay. As it turned out, lo and behold, that sexy ex-pop singer turned preacher wasn't just hot under the collar. The musical minister also sizzled under the sheets. Reporters received an anonymous tip claiming

Reverend Bay had a little Georgia of his own, except Bay's Georgia was alive and healthy, while the reverend's wife—the same woman who loved and supported him through his years of alcohol abuse—was bravely fighting cancer. I often wondered if that anonymous tipper had known about Mrs. Bay's illness. Perhaps they would not have volunteered the information if they had. In any event, it was another stroke of luck for Mark McGregor who recovered as quickly as *Reunion*'s sales.

The publisher was well again, and to celebrate he chose to invest in something that represented spirits of a different kind. An old English pub (Gordo had only seen in pictures) became Mark McGregor's newest acquisition.

Pubs always felt comfortable to me. Sometimes they were cozily quiet. Other times they were lively and filled with wonderful, colorful characters. There wasn't one exactly like the other. However, they all had their charm, and the pub aptly called McGregor's, where I'd agreed to meet Gordo, was no exception. Its high ceilings, shiny brass, and beautifully designed stained-glass windows didn't just make everything feel inviting—the whole thing also brought back a memory of something I used to daydream about as a child. I used to imagine a candle-lit Victorian room with huge cushions comfortably arranged on a cozy white area rug in front of a fireplace. The visual I had created, complete with rustling logs, used to bring me much contentment and joy. It was my special place—always safe—and somehow it felt like McGregor's wooden staircase was about to lead me to it.

I arrived a few minutes early and made my way to the ladies' room to freshen up. The lighting in the bathroom and over the mirror also had its charm. To be more precise, a quick glance in the mirror showed an added glow to my skin and my hair that was pulled back in a ponytail.

Gordo had asked me to meet him in the bar area located on the opposite side of the restaurant dining room. The section was split in two, one part being a cozy lounge with a roaring fire (much like the fireplace I had dreamed of), and the other was a warm and wooden bar section where I sat with a glass of red wine beside a stool that held the latest edition of *Reunion*. The magazine's cover image of two ethereal-like lovers, kissing in the wind, inspired someone—a man who stood behind me—to start a conversation.

Chapter 1

"You would be my goddess," said a gentle soft-speaking voice. I didn't turn around.

"I'm sorry," he continued, "that sounded a little cheesy. I hope I didn't offend you." I wasn't offended, but I also wasn't in the mood for small talk. Actually, I was a little nervous. Even though we spoke warmly to each other on the phone, I didn't know how it was going to go with Gordo. For some reason, I had an uneasy feeling and wanted to take a few deep breaths before he arrived.

I'd heard it said that taking deep breaths is the fastest and easiest way to relax. I'd heard many things about the breath, not just as it relates to one's health, but also that a change in its pattern or an interruption, like a "take your breath away" moment, can indicate the beginning of love. I always balked at such notions. I wasn't much of a romantic. Perhaps my heart couldn't dance that way, or at least that was what I kept telling myself until that evening—until that moment—when the man with the "cheesy line" came into my view. Undiscouraged by my silence, he slipped onto the stool beside me, after removing the magazine. It was unbelievable, really—as if the universe had heard me. I turned around, looked at him, and experienced my first "take your breath away" moment, which was a weird fluttering jumping sensation that almost made me moan.

I guessed he was a bit younger than me, and he looked a little like a hippie. With light-auburn hair that passed his shoulders, he was not my usual type. He was also quite slender and tiny. Even seated, one could tell that he wasn't very tall. However, he had these enormous eyes, doe-like and full of spirit, which left me breathless with awe. "The last thing I wanted to do," he said, "was offend you." Then he said something else, something I wasn't able to hear, and he leaned a little closer. Normally, I wouldn't have liked that. I normally didn't like sitting too close to strangers. But nothing in that moment felt like "normally", and he didn't feel like any stranger. There was something very natural about that moment and something very familiar about that man. A sudden rush of energy made me turn. In fact, I almost jerked my head in the opposite direction, from where Gordo was coming to join us.

Gordo, with his short tight curls and beige khakis, almost reminded me of an ad for *Ralph Lauren*. Looking more like he worked for *Esquire* than

Chapter 1

Reunion, he smiled at me, but addressed the man. He told him he didn't expect to see him. The man sheepishly looked at him and sighed. "The thought of Betsey sitting here alone," he said, "didn't sit well with me, so when you told me you were going to be late, I decided to drop in."

The man asked me if I remembered him. In the end, I did. He looked very different from before. His Gothic pallor was gone. He now had a glowing tan and sun kissed hair that no longer fell into his eyes. It was something in his voice. That's what made me realize who he was, and possibly it was what also made me accidentally push my elbow against my glass of wine—my almost full glass of wine that ultimately landed in my lap. *How mortifying,* one would think. I would have also thought so, had it not been for what happened next, because that was much worse. Somehow in my fluster and haste to get up and clean myself off, I caught my heel on the leg of my barstool and ended up on the floor underneath it. Needless to say, I stirred some attention. The idiot who fell off her stool abruptly seized the eyes of McGregor's whispering patrons. Shocked and humiliated, I closed *my* eyes and briefly considered keeping them tightly shut. I figured if I pretended to be unconscious, someone would inevitably provide me with the perfect escape by calling nine-one-one. But that wasn't meant to be. A second or two later, I opened my eyes in reaction to feeling a warm comforting caress on the left side of my forehead and a soft-sounding voice asking me if I was all right. The voice wasn't Gordo's. Once more, it was Mark McGregor's. The man I had remembered minutes earlier was kneeling by my side, sighing with relief.

"This time, you scared me," he said. "I felt like I was falling too!"

So much kindness shone from his eyes. I held his gaze, and, even in the face of my humiliation, I felt like we were having another moment. For the longest time, I had disdained Mark McGregor. Now, he kept stealing my breath away. Once again, everything seemed surreal.

Chapter 2

I left McGregor's immediately thereafter, despite Mark McGregor's insistence that I stay. A couple of weeks later, I waited in my doctor's examination room for my annual checkup and found myself thinking about that night again. I thought about Gordo whom I hadn't heard from since and who had disappeared immediately after I fell. Perhaps that shouldn't have surprised me. He always did have trouble handling embarrassing situations, unlike Mark McGregor— thinking about him made me sigh. I couldn't believe how different he was from what I had remembered. I supposed the manner in which he abruptly dismissed me that morning at my brother's formed my original perception, and then the events of that fateful, humiliating night completely changed my view.

My general practitioner, Dr. Katz, disrupted my thoughts when he walked into the room. He was a stocky man with a short white beard and a smile that reminded me of Edmund Gwenn as old St. Nick in *Miracle on 34th Street.*

Like usual, that morning, the doctor performed my general checkup before proceeding with the gynecological exam. I had been feeling tenderness in my left breast for about a week, but I was premenstrual, so it didn't at all concern me. I also didn't think it would concern the doctor. The thought that there could be something wrong with me never entered my mind. In fact, my mind was about to drift back to Mark McGregor when Dr. Katz interrupted me again. "Betsey," he said, "what's this?" During my breast examination, the doctor detected something he called suspicious—some sort of abnormality, in my left breast, which could not automatically be attributed to premenstrual hormones. Minutes later, he was on the phone, speaking to another doctor, a surgeon who was his personal friend and who did him a favor by agreeing to see me that same day. In almost an instant, I went from a state of dreamy rumination to feeling as though an octopus crept up inside me, squeezed my heart, and crawled into my throat. It was only when I left the surgeon's office (later that afternoon) that I felt I could breathe again.

The surgeon had told me nine out of ten lumps are nonmalignant, and I thought that with odds like that and no history of cancer in my family, mine had to be benign. Sadly, however, that wasn't the case. A week later I arrived home, from my follow up appointment, holding a little piece of paper that fell from my hand only after my newly adopted yellow Labrador puppy licked my fingers. As the little piece of paper, containing the date and time of my lumpectomy, floated softly to the floor, I thought about how sick I might be and the pain I might have to endure. The more I thought about it, the more frightened I became, and soon I was on the floor beside the paper, yelling—screaming—for my grandmother, telling her, "I need you." By that point, my chest felt like it was about to explode. I couldn't stop shaking. Tears poured from my eyes, yet despite it all, I realized that my grandmother was still very much there. She never quite left me. Her magic was always there. I just chose to stop believing it. I chose to stop myself from feeling it. I loved Nana with all my heart, but a part of me didn't want to be like her. As I grew older, it seemed that where I came from never quite fit in with where I thought I wanted to be. Ultimately, I suppressed the believer, the mystic, in me, and in the process I lost my way. I got lost when it came to love and broke my promise to my grandmother by becoming emotionally constricted. The world Nana had tried to make me see was very different from what's commonly termed "the real world". Or, again, more accurately, was it not I who one day decided that? After a couple of disappointments, was I not the one who decided to harden my heart and stop believing that the two worlds could ever interchange. My brain couldn't stop spinning. *How many times,* I wondered, *had magic come to find me?* How many times had it stared me in the face? I think subconsciously I always yearned for it and for my soul twin, whose presence I could sometimes almost feel. My thoughts raced back and forth between the possibility of my dying sooner than I ever expected and regrets about the magic I felt I missed. In an effort to pull myself together and control my racing thoughts, I focused on a small light, fixed beneath my kitchen counter. The tiny bulb was about to burn out, which I assumed was the reason it reflected an odd, almost fluorescent-green hue. *It's funny,* I thought, *how peace can come from something as simple as a little light. Magic!* I smiled. There it was. In the midst of my tornado, that tiny bulb magically distracted me into a reprieve.

My mother, who lived in Vermont, drove down on the night before my surgery. It meant the world to me to have her there—her and my brother. Both of them being there, for me and with me, reduced my fear to a more manageable level.

The lumpectomy itself didn't take longer than forty minutes. Before I knew it, I was awake and chatting with my mother and John who were also in the room with me when the surgeon came to deliver some very good news. My cancer had not spread to my lymph nodes. It was caught early. I was cancer free. What a feeling that was! Elation, relief, and wonder captured the sudden change in my life. And then, just as quickly, everything changed again.

Three days following my surgery, right before I was to be released from the hospital, I contracted pneumonia. Four days after that, the chest pain was so sharp I thought I was going die. On the eighth night of my hospital stay, my mother and brother, neither of whom left me alone since I'd contracted the infection, finally went home to get some rest. The doctor on staff assured them I would sleep through the night. He didn't foresee my fever rising again. Yet later that night, it had me delirious, as I woke up, calling once more for my grandmother and then thinking she was the nurse who ran into my room before I drifted back to sleep. That was the last thing I remembered before waking again after feeling a light kiss on my forehead. Fevers certainly do strange things. Nobody was there, but strangely, when I woke up the next morning, my fever was gone, almost as if someone had kissed it away.

I didn't require any follow-up cancer treatments, only a short recovery period, after which my doctors gave me a clean bill of health. Thank God! I felt like He had given me a second chance, following a wake-up call.

I might have stopped believing in magic, but never did I stop praying to God. I had always been one who talked to God, even if I no longer knew how to pay attention for answers of divine guidance. I tried, I guess, at one time, to reopen those magical divine channels from which answers flow. That was through a six-week comprehensive meditation course, a couple of years earlier. However, it had not managed to stick. Actually, I hadn't managed to stick with it. I had struggled to find my stillness at that course. There, we were taught to count our breaths and repeat certain mantras, which might have been the problem. It seemed meditation proved challenging to me because of the way I kept fighting to clear my mind. I had compared it to a wrestling match with nothingness, not having comprehended that, for me, meditation should never have been about shutting things out.

Indian spiritual master and author, Meher Baba, wrote, *We have three distinct types of meditation. In the first type of meditation the intellect is predominantly brought into play; it might be called "discriminative meditation." In the second type the heart is predominantly brought into play; it might be called the "meditation of the heart." In the third type the active nature of man is predominantly brought into play; it might be called "the meditation of action." Discriminative meditation is represented by intellectual assertion of a formula like "I am not my body, but the Infinite." The meditation of the heart is represented by a steady and unhampered flow of love from the aspirant to the Divine Beloved. The meditation of action is represented by an unreserved dedication of one's life to the selfless service of the Master or humanity. Of these three types, meditation of the heart is the highest and most important, but the other two types also have their own value and cannot be neglected without serious detriment to the spiritual progress of the aspirant.*

I didn't know that at the time—that there were different types of meditation. Nor did I know that the one for me was of the heart. I hadn't read what Meher Baba said. However, somehow, post-surgery, while once again fighting to clear my mind after deciding to give meditation another go, I had an "aha moment" where I realized the difference between a thought from the brain and a feeling from the heart. That was it! That was my breakthrough. Almost instantly I understood that if I wanted to meditate I needed to change my focus from my mind to my heart. It was simple, really. Rather than fighting to cease from thinking, I began to concentrate. I concentrated on what I was feeling— in my body and in my breath. It truly was very simple, yet at the same time it was also powerful; so powerful that it led me to be more aware of my prana—my life force. And it allowed me to let that energy lead me into peace. Finally, I found my place in meditation;

or, that was, for the most part, because I also came to realize that no two experiences were ever exactly the same. I mainly felt grounded and serene when I meditated, but there were also times when sadness would ensue, and I didn't always know why. Sometimes all I knew was that I had to observe the feeling and permit it to well up in me. As uncomfortable as it might have been, I had to allow myself to feel it. My grandmother used to say that every soul has a story. Seemingly, I was tapping into mine.

My deepening spiritual practice inspired me to wake earlier one morning. That particular Sunday, I rose before the sun. I was anxious to meditate that day. Almost as soon as I got up, I placed cushions in front of my living room window. I then closed my eyes and sensed the room grow brighter. By the end of that meditation, the sun had fully risen, and I felt an unusual urge, almost like a pull, to go outside. The last time I had taken a good long walk outdoors seemed like forever ago. My dog, Max, and I would go for quick jaunts around the block, but since my surgery, I had not been able to go much farther. Being outside tended to make me dizzy; however, at the same time, I knew I wasn't going to regain the rest of my strength without some real movement in the fresh air. At last, I decided to give it a try and embarked with Max on a lengthy stroll in Central Park.

As usual on Sunday mornings, the park was filled with people—joggers, walkers, and cyclists. It all felt so wonderful, and I loved New York for that. That city has its own special brand of magic. No other place can make you feel so alive. Even the leaves came back to life. They had begun to adorn the park's grounds and some danced together in the wind. I stopped for a minute to watch them. They swirled and jumped, loving the cool sunny breeze—another form of magic—that eventually sent one of them fluttering to my foot. *Everything is connected,* I thought, *everyone and everything, including this little leaf.* Nana once said that maple leaves are very special. Like those of a palm of a person's hand, their lines hold secrets of untold tales. I picked up the leaf and twirled it by the stem, between my fingers. It certainly did have its share of lines. Also, it was very colorful. The bright yellow in its center traveled toward its edges and seemed to warm the palm of *my* hand, as I glided through the rest of the autumn foliage.

Max and I slowly made our way to Strawberry Fields, where I had never been before and where I thought I heard someone call my name. At first, I didn't see anyone, but then when I heard "Betsey" a second time, I couldn't believe my eyes. Nothing could have stopped me from recognizing him, not this time. This time, even with his bicycle helmet strapped on, I knew him instantly. In yet another surreal moment, I watched him kick down the stand of his bicycle, swing off his bike, remove his helmet, and take hold of my arm. He said he was feeling "a little breathless" and apparently needed my arm to steady himself until an unfathomable dizzy spell suddenly caused *me* to need his support. To my horror, that surreal moment transformed into a humiliating instance of déjà vu. The only thing that made it different from the last time was that, on this occasion, Mark McGregor was the breathless one. And he caught me. This time he stopped me from hitting the ground.

Mark secured me by the waist with his arm and led me to a nearby bench where I sat with my face in my hands.

"Betsey, look at me," he said, after tying Max's leash to the bench. "Please. Tell me you're all right."

I used to run six miles every day, and now a walk almost knocked me out. *How could that be all right?* I felt frail, frightened, and inept. I felt anything but all right.

He then squatted down in front me, and I started to cry. "Let it out," he said. "That's good. It's good to cry. Crying is a gift that heals the soul."

"I wish my body would heal," I said, after taking a few deep breaths. "I'm sorry. I had surgery not too long ago."

"I know you did." He sighed. "But listen, be gentle with yourself. These things take time."

Once again, his eyes were filled with kindness and also with a wisdom that seemed to surpass his years.

"You are an old soul." I smiled.

"We all are," he replied. "Our lessons are different, but we are all the same."

At that moment, I wanted to hug him. In fact, I almost did. He must have known it, too, because he quickly rose from his squatted position, sat beside me, and pressed me close.

Chapter 3

By the time December came around, I was finally feeling healthy and working part time, acting in commercials. Admittedly, my jobs were limited, but they were also well-paying, so I didn't mind. I liked the free time they afforded. It gave me the opportunity to try my hand at something new. I wasn't focusing on starting a new career (at least not yet), but I was beginning to find truth in what C.S. Lewis once said about writing being a great cure for all human ills.

Christmas came and went in a flash that year. I celebrated with John, our mother, and our extended family in Vermont. With Max in tow, we drove up on the twenty-fourth, but then headed back to New York on the twenty-sixth, because John was anxious to return.

John was in charge of *Reunion*'s New Year's Eve party at McGregor's and had last-minute details to arrange. He was pumped about that party, so much so he excitedly invited me. I hadn't been to McGregor's in forever, not since the night of my humiliating fall; and I hadn't seen Mark McGregor—not since that day in Central Park. That day, we ended up spending the entire afternoon together, after which he walked me home, gave me his numbers, and asked me to call him; but I never did. At the time, I didn't have the strength to start anything new. However, I never stopped thinking about him. Even while John was speaking to me about the party, my mind was on something that happened that afternoon when Mark and I were still cozily sitting on our bench. It was something rather remarkable. A raven—a bird almost never seen in New York City—had landed near my foot, leaving Mark in awe. He said it was a sign and then smiled when I cringed. "What I mean," he explained, "is that this bird, right here, right now, is a good sign. Ravens are reputed to be bad omens, but they're not. They only scare us because of made-up stories—fables that cloud our minds. So many think of ravens in a negative way, but actually they are very loving birds. Did you know that ravens have very few natural predators, or that they are romantic? Oh yes!" His smile widened. "Ravens are very romantic. They often fly with wingtips touching, and at any time of the year, pairs can be found sitting in a tree, side by side, cooing to each other, and using their long heavy beaks to kiss." Then, or rather at the word "kiss", he touched my nose with his finger and melted my heart with his enormous emerald green eyes.

"Earth to Betsey, Earth to Betsey, report in!" John's voice barreled through my thoughts. "You didn't answer me. What do you think?" he said. "Would you like to come to the party? It would mean a lot to me to have you there."

I looked at him and smiled. "Can I ask you something?"

"Sure." He smiled back. "You can ask me anything you want, after you answer *my* question." The twinkle in his eyes was back. He was worshipped for it in his teenage years. *Soulful eyes*, they used call him. Then, three years ago, he lost it, assumedly due to what had been happening to *Reunion* and his boss.

"Yes," I said. "I would love to."

"That's the answer I was looking for," he laughed. "Ok, go ahead now. Ask away."

I felt a little awkward about bringing it up to John. However, that didn't stop me. There was something I really had to know. "One night, Mark was sick," I said, "Gordo phoned me…"

My brother's eyes instantly widened, though not really in surprise. In fact, if I read him correctly, my bringing it up seemed to please him. "I know," he said.

"You do?"

"I do. I was there too. What would you like to know?"

"I'd like to know what happened. What was wrong with Mark?"

"What was wrong with him and what happened are two different things."

"Gordo sounded panicked that night. And he never sounds panicked."

Chapter 3

"Indeed," John said. "It was a worrying situation. Mark wouldn't eat. He couldn't focus on his work. He suffered from fatigue, dizziness, headaches, and nausea. He'd become so frail, so weak, and then that night, he collapsed. He had just come out of the hospital after having undergone further tests. He was staying at Gordo's. Like I said, I was there, as well. Gordo had invited me for supper, and the three of us were about to sit at the table when Mark received a phone call that I can only assume was responsible for aggravating his already high level of anxiety—aggravating it to the point where he passed out while standing at the top of the basement stairs. Thank God, Gordo was there to catch him. Had he not, Mark would have likely broken his neck."

"Thank God," I repeated. "Did you call nine-one-one?"

"No." John sighed. "We didn't. Mark wasn't unconscious for more than half a minute. By the time Gordo got him to the couch, he had already come to and was adamantly against us calling nine-one-one. He was scared. He had just gone through all these tests and was told that all was well physically, but perhaps not emotionally. Doctors suspected severe emotional and psychological stress, stemming from events of that past year, which included a violent attack outside our office building. To make a long story shorter, they proceeded by recommending an evaluation for anxiety, depression, etc., and Mark refused. He told me, 'They're not finding what's wrong with me, and I feel powerless, helpless—absolutely helpless!' He begged us not to call nine-one-one on the night of his collapse because he was afraid of landing in a loony bin. That was why we didn't call. But then, almost immediately after, Mark stopped talking. He wouldn't respond to anything we'd say. He became so catatonic; I was afraid he might have somehow hit his head on the wall, or something, before Gordo caught him."

"Gordo thought I could help him, but John, at the time, I didn't—"

"I was the one who suggested he call you."

"*You* did? Why?"

"It was a feeling—an instinct I had. Betsey, Mark liked you so much. He loved watching you on TV. He thought you were perfect. Once, on an off day, he told me your smile raised his vibrations. I don't know what to say—a part of me believed him."

I was silently thanking God and whichever angel inspired me to go to Gordo's house that night. It didn't matter that no one knew I was there. At that moment, after hearing those words, the only thing that mattered was that I knew I was there, because if I wouldn't have charged through the rain that night, my heart would now be in pieces.

"In any case," John said, "the next morning, Mark appeared to have breathed in new life. He was still shaky. I think a leaf could have knocked him down. However, his attitude had completely changed. He was apologetic, gracious, and positive. He assured us he was going to be fine. He said all he needed was a little bit of time to get his strength back, and we told him to take whatever time he wanted. We promised him we would hold down the fort at work, to which he returned six weeks later, right as rain."

"How has he been since then?"

"Since then, Betsey," John smiled widely, "I am happy to report that Mark has been just fine. He works the same outrageous hours he's always done, and when he's not working, he's probably watching taped episodes of your soap."

"Come on, John!" The thought of that made me laugh. "So many beautiful women pose for that magazine, and you think he spends his time watching clips of me? Mark must have a slew of girlfriends."

"No," he laughed. "Not one. Mark hasn't had a girlfriend for as long as I've known him. These girls are his magazine's models. They work for him. It's all business. No," John repeated. "Mark is holding out for his special love. He believes a special love exists for everyone. He says it's not always obvious and most of us give up before we ever find it, yet in our hearts we feel it, because that person, whether he or she is known to us or not, is, in a way, part of our DNA— our energetic DNA, our soul signature. Have you ever had a dream lover?"

"A what?"

"A dream lover," he said, "someone stemming from your day or nighttime dreams?"

"No," I replied, but the truth was I didn't want to share. First, I thought it was too personal, and second, I had only just begun to consciously explore and understand that part of my subconscious. As much as

Georgia Snow lived out her fantasies of playing the victim, I used to quietly dream about rescuing. I was the hero in my fantasies, while my dream lover, who was quite different from the qualities I normally presented to the world, was someone I needed to protect. Through meditation, visualization, dream analysis, and a little creative writing, I had started to get to know the trusting fragile essence that often came to me in my fantasies and my dreams, and somehow, it was making me feel more and more complete.

John then mentioned what Carl Jung wrote in *The Development of Personality*. In his book, Dr. Jung stated that *every man carries within him the eternal image of woman, not the image of this or that particular woman, but a definite feminine image.* My brother went on to say that the dream lover is an image that never really goes away, "or, at east, not too far away...

"What I mean," he said, "is that this image often remains in our subconscious, the unconscious mind, which is why we don't normally connect our attractions to it. All our attractions, to varying degrees, give us the opportunity to see different aspects of ourselves in other people, but it is through our most powerful pulls that we get glimpses of our *eternal* image—of that very intimate part of ourselves. In other words, your dream lover—your eternal image—is really a part of you. You can recognize it in another person. It's what makes another compatible to you. However, the foundation of that image—its root—is in your psyche."

"I do understand," I said. "But as far as Mark goes—"

"Listen, that *is* as far as Mark goes. He's not a virgin, but as far as relationships are concerned, he is holding out for the one. He told me that finding that person, uniting with that person—the one who can make you want to live your days again and again—*is* something he feels everyone should wait for. Betsey, he's a good man with a gentle soul. A little floufy perhaps..."

"Floufy?" I'd never heard that word before.

"I mean he's not afraid to wear the sheer nylon socks he orders from England...No," he chuckled, "what I really mean is that he's got a highly developed feminine side. Mark's creative, talkative, and kind. And he's sensitive. He even cries over sad movies, which is one of the reasons I feel he would be perfect for you."

Chapter 3

"Why? Because I cry over sad movies?"

"Do you?"

"What do you mean?"

"Just that you should give him a chance—that I think you would complement one another. I never thought anyone would be good enough for you, but Mark is. He prayed for you day and night when you were ill. I *love* you, Betsey—I want you to be happy. You deserve to be happy. You both do."

"But John?" I smiled.

"I feel it, Betsey. I don't know why exactly. I can't explain it. I just feel it, and I think Mark does too. Life can be very simple that way, simple and beautiful. We are the ones who make it complicated. We are the ones who tarnish its beauty by trying to analyze and control everything we feel. If only now and then we could allow our sixth sense to take over. If only now and then we could allow ourselves to feel—just feel."

I had never heard my brother speak that way before. I stared at him in silence (and a little in awe) until my next question could no longer remain unasked. "What do you mean that Mark does too?"

"Mark is in love with you."

"Oh, come on," I exclaimed.

"Oh, yeah! Every time I mention your name, his eyes start looking like Bambi's. And by the way"—John smiled—"he cried watching *Bambi*."

"I don't believe you."

"God's honest truth. I was with him."

"No, silly, I mean about him being in love with me."

"Well, you can believe what you want, but I'm not kidding. This is one of those instances that doesn't require further analysis."

Admittedly, not everything John said came as a surprise. The memory of being with Mark that day in Central Park, feeling his soft warm breath upon my skin while we sat almost glued together on that bench, kept tugging at my heart.

John had mentioned that Mark never had a girl-friend, but then I thought, *what about Georgia Snow?* What about his relationship with her? Surely, John must have known of it. Once more, I couldn't stop myself from asking; yet, as soon as I did, I wanted to take it back. I wanted to not have said it the moment I saw the twinkle in his eyes once again fade away. "No," he said. "No, Georgia wasn't Mark's girlfriend. She was—or rather, she started out as our receptionist and quickly became a vital part of *my* life.

"What can I say? She was so beautiful," he exclaimed. "She was so full of spirit! Gigi, which was what I always called her, started working at the magazine at the same time I did, and we instantly connected. We had so much fun together. We'd have lunch, cof-fee. We even joined a book club. I talked and shared with her, unlike any friendship I'd ever had before. In retrospect, she was what made me truly under-stand Mark's philosophy, because something about her made me feel so much more like me. "Betsey, I would have done anything for her, and now I can't help but feel that my overzealousness to please her contributed to her death." He then pulled over to the side of the road and rolled down his window, letting a breeze of cool air blow through. It felt so refreshing, I thought—almost like someone was lovingly touching my cheek. John was also feeling it and breathing it. He took a few calming breaths and then continued to speak. "Gigi wanted to model," he said. "Modeling had been her dream. She talked about it often; so often that I couldn't help but encourage her by suggesting that she slightly change her look and by convincing Mark to give her a chance to pose for *Reunion*. I really had to talk him into it. For whatever reason, it didn't feel right to him. How I wish I had agreed. If I would have, she would still be here, and Mark would have been saved a lot of grief. But I didn't agree, nor did I listen to anything he had to say. Instead, I pushed him until he gave in, which resulted in Gigi receiving all kinds of offers for print, music videos, and TV. I was so proud of her. Following our shoot, everybody wanted her. In one blink of an eye she was on top of the world, and in another she was gone."

"John—"

"It was all my fault."

"No, it wasn't."

Chapter 3

"Yes, Betsey, it was. She wasn't equipped to handle it. Emotionally it proved to be too much. She got caught up in the partying. She started using cocaine. I knew something was wrong. There were signs, many signs, including the time she called me in the middle of the night. That night, she said she had fallen and felt a little woozy. When I got there, she was lying on her bedroom floor. Apparently, she was afraid to get up, fearing a dizzy spell, but like Mark, she begged me not to call nine-one-one. She said she had slipped and was a little dazed by the fall. However, she insisted she wasn't hurt. And that was how she looked. She appeared to be uninjured. At the time, I believed her. Now, I can't believe how foolish that was. Things could have turned out much differently had I made that call."

I squeezed John's hand and told him it wouldn't have mattered, but he insisted that it could have—that they might have detected her drug use. "And who knows," he said, "maybe she didn't slip. All I know is that she was weak and frightened."

"John, it wasn't your fault." I remembered what I had read about Georgia, including her pre-*Reunion* addiction to cocaine. As a result, I did my best to remind him, ever so gently, that Georgia's problems started long before she met him.

"I loved her, Betsey. I did, you know. I loved her with all my heart." His eyes were almost drowning in tears. "She shouldn't have died like that," he said, "nor should she be remembered as anything other than the beautiful girl she was."

"Well how do you remember her?" I asked. "You described her as beautiful with lots of spirit, which means her true self managed to shine through, at least it did to you. You got see the real Georgia, didn't you? Her problems and addictions didn't hide her essence from you."

My brother reached out and hugged me. A lump rose in my throat. "Betsey," he sighed, "I never told her how much I truly loved her. I wish I could go back!"

"Maybe you still can."

"What do you mean?"

At that moment, I remembered my grandmother looking at the sky. When John asked her about his twin soul all those years ago, she pointed to the stars and told him to also look in between. Time and again I might have tried, but always there was a part of me that could never completely dispel psychic phenomena or eternal life. Something within me always pulled me back to believing, though never quite as strongly as it did at that particular instant when a rise of energy inspired me to tell him what to do. "When you get home," I said, "buy flowers, like you are buying them for her, then put on some soft romantic music, light candles, and sit comfortably, relaxing your body and your mind. Allow your attention to focus inward. Notice what you're feeling, physically and emotionally, and let your thoughts arise and fall freely. In other words, don't chase your thoughts away, but don't linger on them either. Let them come. Let them go. And, eventually, they will bring you to a place of surrender from where you can begin to visualize Georgia. Her hair is waving through the air. Her eyes look like sapphires in the light. And her smile is as fresh as it was the very first time you saw it. Then, as that visualization gets clearer, look at her facing you and allow the love you feel for her to envelope you. Take your time with this experience. Breathe deeply. Imagine her chest almost touching yours and send loving energy from your heart to hers. Don't try to force the energy. Don't attempt to control the emotion it triggers. Just let it flow—believe, breathe, feel. Like you said, sometimes you just have to feel."

Chapter 4

As the New Year quickly approached, so did *Reunion*'s party. I was starting to feel a little nervous about it and was thinking about what to wear when my brother's assistant, Carol Cheetham, called, reminding me about my hair. Carol was about my age, and by then, she had worked with my brother for almost three years. Prior to that, she had lived through an abusive marriage that had driven her and her daughter to flee. Life hadn't been easy for Carol. After leaving her husband, she and her pre-teen daughter were forced live in a shelter—that was, until the day she bumped into Mark McGregor by chance. Like Gordo and me, Carol and Mark had been friends in high school, but unlike Gordo and me, they'd lost touch. That chance meeting, a few years earlier, was the first time they'd seen each other since school. It was also the first time Carol had revealed her situation to someone outside of the shelter. "We all have angels," she once told me, "both the ethereal kind and humans, who are kind, like Mark McGregor." Mark and Carol's serendipitous meeting that day resulted in him offering her a job that helped her get back on her feet. Strangely, Carol and I became acquainted since also meeting by chance. We both shared the same hair salon, where through casual chatter one evening, while having our hair colored, we discovered my brother was her boss. Since then, we often met at the salon, which was actually what prompted her to call me two days before *Reunion*'s party. She'd found out I was going and wanted to know if I had made an appointment for my hair.

My hair wasn't difficult to do. Long and plentiful, I would wash and wear it by putting it up in a bun and then letting it down once it dried. It would fall quite nicely that way, shiny, with loose waves cascading down to the middle of my back. I would rarely have it blow dried, not even for special occasions. However, every now and then I would have it dyed. I was naturally an ash blond color, which was something I never strayed too far from. As much as I had loved trying different looks when I was younger, I now liked to keep my hair looking healthy through regular conditioning treatments, trims, and occasional blonder highlights.

Carol and I ultimately arranged to meet at our mutual salon to freshen our locks on the morning of *Reunion*'s New Year's Eve soiree. Our coloring processes—my streaks and her usual dye job—took about an hour to complete, after which we were shampooed, seated in the front of the place, and informed that our stylist would soon join us. We also shared the same stylist who eventually emerged from the back. Kenneth, a tiny Hawaiian man, gave phenomenal cuts, but his bedside manner, so to speak, unfortunately left much to be desired. He often poked fun at me, sometimes cruelly, and I sort of believed his behavior stemmed from my refusal to allow him to get creative with my hair—that and the fact that he might have caught on to how the sound of his voice always made me want to laugh. He had an insanely imitated French accent that sounded so comical, it overshadowed anything he had to say. Every time he spoke, I would fight not to chuckle, but this time was different. This time, remarks such as "You can't possibly be thinking of keeping the same cut. Batsee, gooood Lord, look in the mirroar. Honee, twenty-five is long done" bothered me.

I thought we would never get out of that place and away from Kenneth's voice, but at last, after another good haircut that was almost worth the abuse, we left and headed off to Macy's, scouring for the ultimate New Year's Eve party dress. Within minutes of entering the store, Carol found what she wanted— what she had envisioned. I, unfortunately, wasn't as successful. Nothing I tried on seemed right. The person I saw in the Macy's changing room mirror looked much older and a little fatter than the one who had not yet heard Kenneth's words. That afternoon, New York City's sidewalks were buzzing with people looking at storefront windows. I wasn't alone. However, in the end, I chose to head back to my place, deciding to shop instead in my own closet. Almost all the way home I thought about what I could wear. Then, right when my options began to look bleak, I stopped, or more precisely I was stopped by another storefront window. Both beauty and perfection (for they do not always go hand in hand) suddenly called to me from a small corner shop boutique that miraculously displayed exactly what I wanted. Right in the center of its window stood my perfect little black dress.

John was to fetch Carol at seven o'clock and me at seven fifteen. I took my time getting ready and then turned to the mirror for a final glance. That vintage-style little black dress really was just right. Haltered at the top and tailored at the hips, it fit me like a glove. The memory of Kenneth's comments had all but faded, and I reflected upon how I had allowed his words to upset me. I also, at the same time and quite unexpectedly, remembered a dream. It had been years since I paid attention to dreams, years since I had one worth paying attention to. Freud called them "the royal road to the unconscious," which made sense to me, because like the effect of Kenneth's comments, the recent dream I recollected could have been brought on by the growing uneasiness I felt about attending *Reunion's* party. I was certain the place would be overflowing with beautiful young women, and perhaps I feared to see one on Mark McGregor's arm. In any event, my dream was about a very beautiful woman. She was indeed quite beautiful, but not like most of the girls in the magazines. No, her beauty went deeper than that. Through the carefree energy of her movements and eyes that were full of spirit and life, her beauty expressed her soul and began to remind me of myself.

McGregor's was decked out in full holiday style: Colored paper and tinsel, adorned with holly, decorated its massive walls, crimson glowed from hundreds of lights, and the fireplace cheerily burned. Carol, John, and I headed closer toward that warm fire. Apparently, our table was near the fireplace, but to get there, we first had to make our way past a crowd of guests that included my old friend, Gordo. I had neither seen nor spoken to Gordo since the night of my humiliating fall. Soon after, I was diagnosed with breast cancer, operated on, and then deathly ill with pneumonia, yet throughout all of it, he remained silent. I wasn't sure if he was going to speak to me now, and I guess, that by saying "Great to see you and take care," he really didn't.

A couple of hours later I caught sight of him again when it was time for the speeches. That was also when I finally saw Mark. Dressed in a tuxedo—one that fit his slender frame so perfectly—Mark stood up to give the last speech of the night, which started with a quote from Woodrow Wilson.

Mark quoted Wilson as saying, "*We grow great by dreams. All big men are dreamers. They see things in the soft haze of a spring day or in the red fire of a long winter's evening. Some of us let these great dreams die, but others nourish and protect them, nurse them through bad days till they bring them to the sunshine and light, which comes always to those who sincerely hope that their dreams will come true.*'" He then turned his head in my direction, and for a moment, I could have sworn he looked at me. "Dreams do come true." He smiled softly. "If you set the intention and believe in something with all your heart, it will happen. Einstein was once credited with saying, '*Everything is energy and that's all there is to it. Match the frequency of the reality you want and you cannot help but get that reality. It can be no other way. This is not philosophy. This is physics.*' As it turned out, this quote was not Albert Einstein's. It belonged to author Darryl Anka, but that doesn't make it less true."

When Mark finished speaking, the applause was overwhelming. One after another, people rose from their seats, eventually making their way toward him, and I followed suit. I wanted to tell him how much I loved his words—how much they touched and inspired me—but I never got the chance. As soon as he saw me coming, he wobbled through the crowd, grabbed my hand, and led me to the dance floor. It was exactly half an hour before midnight. The DJ had started to play an intimate slow song when Mark wrapped his arms around me, smiled into my eyes, and said, "This is *my* dream." He said, "This is it."

Impulsiveness had never been one of my character traits, especially when it came to men. I could not be easily roused and was certainly not one to take any action. In fact, I had never made a first move in my life—not until I heard those words and looked into those wise green eyes that for a moment seemed so vulnerable. My hands rested on his shoulders. Slowly, I raised them to the back of his neck. This made him shiver—just for a second he quivered—right before I kissed him. I kissed him with a passion that made him swoon.

"Oh," he whispered. "Hold me. You just swept me off my feet! I was so busy thinking of ways to woo you that I never once imagined you would be wooing me."

We remained in each other's arms and continued to dance long after everyone else had left. Then, finally,

Chapter 4

at the crack of dawn, Mark collapsed onto the big leather couch in front of that warm fire and pulled me down with him. He smiled, as did I at him, to myself, and to the universe when I thought about the time I danced like a wild child at a schoolmate's birthday party. Everybody laughed at me at that party. I was so embarrassed; I couldn't bring myself to really dance again. I couldn't bring myself to let that incident go. It's funny how life is. For as long as I wanted to, I couldn't, and then in Mark's arms, I forgot it ever happened.

Chapter 5

I was still nestled in Mark's arms when I woke up a couple of hours later to a rather abrupt realization. My beloved dog, Max, most likely needed to pee. I gently nudged Mark who stretched out and yawned. "Canine responsibilities," I chuckled. "I have to go."

Smiling sleepily, Mark fixed his eyes upon me almost like he had not quite awakened from a dream. "I'm coming too," he said and then looked at me in a way that seemed to indicate a momentary loss of confidence. Those beautiful green eyes were now wide open. And I smiled too. How could he think that I wouldn't want him with me?

The circumstances at my place were happier than anticipated. Max was going nuts, but at least he had not peed. I threw off my wrinkled party dress and changed into jeans and a sweater. Mark had already showered and dressed at a small flat he kept above McGregor's.

It was a sunny New Year's Day. We walked for a long while, enjoying the coolness of the air. The snow was fresh and white. Silver slivers sparkled in the sun. Tiny diamonds, one by one, reminded me of winters in Alberta. On the first snowfall of every year, my grandmother would bundle up my brother and me and then take us outside to make snow angels. For a moment, I imagined myself lying with her in the snow once again, laughing with delight, moving my arms up and down and my legs from side to side. When I was a child, I believed in angels and thought that snowdrifts were heavenly clouds borrowed from the angels for a few long months every year. I never thought of heaven as being a faraway place. I was certain the two worlds regularly interchanged. How else could one explain the magic of Christmas or the budding beauty of spring? How else could one explain the way every season made us feel? True magic connects to us from the outside in and the inside out. That's how I knew heaven was real. When I was a child, I found signs of it everywhere. But then, that slowly went away. Little by little, I closed that part of my vision until meditation and writing helped me open it again and helped me *feel* again— feel the breath of heaven like I did that morning through the cool air on my skin, the warm memory of my grandmother, and the touch of Mark's hand holding mine.

The next day, Mark was supposed to have supper at his mother's, and he insisted that I come with him. Some might have considered this to be a little soon. However, I agreed instantly. I wanted to know everything about him.

Shirley McGregor lived three hours away from New York City in a small scenic area where commodious houses with bright red doors, built well before most of us were born, captured my imagination. Looking at them from the outside had me picturing all sorts of cozy delights, including enormous mugs filled with steaming hot chocolate.

"Mark, this is beautiful," I said. "Is this where you're from?"

"No." He looked at me quickly and smiled. "God, no. But my mother used to bring me here when I was a child. We'd go to the beach and the amusement park. It was always so much fun. She dreamed of living in this neighborhood, and now she does."

Shirley McGregor's home was a little smaller, but just as picturesque as the rest. A white two-story cottage, it sat at the corner of a quiet block that was momentarily disturbed by Mrs. McGregor herself when she opened the door to greet us. "Happy New Year!" shouted the beautiful blond woman who looked more like she could have been Mark's sister. Tall, slender, tanned, and very blond, she had cheekbones as high and eyes as wide as Mark's.

After exchanging introductions and warm holiday hugs, the three of us sat together in Mrs. McGregor's sun-filled living room, clinking glasses of Australian merlot. Eventually, Mark left the room to set the table for supper. "He loves helping me," beamed his mother. "He has ever since he was a little boy.

"I used to worry about him. Life wasn't easy for him. He had to fight from the moment he was born." I didn't know what she talking about. I was not at all

Chapter 5

familiar with his childhood. Lowering my glass, I listened as she explained. "Mark was four months premature." She sighed. "Doctors were sure he was going to die. Even if he did survive, they said the odds were that he'd be battling medical problems his entire life. His lungs were underdeveloped. Oxygen helped him breathe. He also needed several blood transfusions. But he didn't give up. He was as feisty then as he is now, and he pulled through. My baby beat the odds and grew into a healthy wonderful young man!

"He is my only child," she said, looking at me warmly. "My husband left us soon after Mark was born." Her hands were on her lap, one was folded over the other. I reached out, touched the top one, and told her I was sorry. "It's not your fault, love." She smiled. "And I'm the one who's sorry. I think that I wasn't very clear. Mark's father isn't dead, or at least not that I'm aware of. No." She sighed again. "A wife and child—especially a sick child—weren't for him. So, it was just Mark and me, and that poor little boy was alone so much of the time. I had to work two jobs to make ends meet. More often than not, he was on his own, but he never complained. In fact, he did the opposite. There was nothing but goodness in him. He always concentrated on positive activities and kept out of trouble by immersing himself in books. They were his companions—the characters he read about and further imagined."

It broke my heart to think of Mark being that alone. Even though his mother insisted that, as much as she worried, he was happy and well adjusted, I got a picture of a frightened little boy. I excused myself, saying I needed to go to the bathroom, but what I really wanted to do was sneak into the dining room to see him. He gave me the biggest smile when I walked in, and I gave him the biggest hug.

When Mark and I arrived back at my place, he took Max for a walk, and I lit the fireplace before taking a shower. Mark and Max weren't gone very long. By the time I got out of the bathroom, they were both lying on the large plush rug in the middle of the living room floor. Mark was scratching Max's belly. Max pawed the air in bliss. "He just loves that," I laughed.

"Of course he does!" Mark laughed too. "Wouldn't you? I mean if you couldn't scratch your own belly."

That night, Mark appeared much like he did the first time I met him at my brother's, with hair hiding his eyes. He looked at me through unruly messy strands, while Max scampered away. "You're a hippie," I said and then joined him on the soft, sprawling rug.

"I am," he replied. "I am a quiet spiritual pagan who has fallen hopelessly and helplessly in love with you."

I took his hair into my hands, pulled it back, and kissed him on the forehead. "Ah," he said, with eyes gleaming, "a forehead kiss. What exactly does that mean?" I wanted to tell him it meant that I was in love with him too, but I didn't. I didn't say anything. Instead, I reflected on how we hadn't yet made love. I had been a little self-conscious about the surgical scar on my breast. However, as Mark continued to look at me, I knew it wasn't going to matter. I knew that scar would be visible only to me. Mark then kissed *me* on the forehead and traced my face with his hand. My temples, my nose, and my cheeks were being lovingly stroked until a tear fell from his eye. I rolled to my side, surprised. He looked at me and smiled. "Nothing's wrong," he whispered. "Everything is just so perfect." Hair fell to his face again. The candles made the lighter strands shine. *He* shined. Mark was as beautiful outside as he was in. Again, he wasn't a big man. His ankles were fine, his legs lean and lanky, and his hips slender. He was delicate in many ways, yet something made him perfect for me—a perfect manifestation of my *eternal* image who brought out the lover in me. Suddenly, the lover I always hoped I could be—caring and kind and passionate and strong—magically came to life. My feminine energy was fully evoked through our magnificent flow of movement and touch, which ultimately ended in a mutual and simultaneous euphoric orgasm.

From that night on, Mark and I were inseparable. We lived at my place and spent every free minute together. If he had to work late or go to some unavoidable function, one which I thought I wouldn't enjoy, I'd wait up for him, passing the time reading or doing homework for the literature program I'd enrolled in at NYU.

I also started seeing more of my brother, whom I often met for drinks or supper or both. At the same time, I became closer to Carol. She and I extended our friendship from the occasional salon chatter to frequent drinks at the pub. "You know, Betsey," Carol said to me once over a bottle of delicious white wine at McGregor's, "you look like you're twenty-two."

"That's how I feel," I said. "I am so utterly in love."

"Be careful." She sighed. "Sometimes, we find ourselves wanting to believe in fairytales again, because, for whatever reason, we want to go backward. We want to return to a certain place from our past."

I took a sip of wine, thought about it for a moment, and wondered how being in love could ever be about going backward. True love, after all, is a powerfully driving force. When I remembered a time from my past—a time of enchantment—and sometimes found myself thinking about those early years that were filled with my grandmother's magic, it wasn't because I wanted to return to a certain place from my past. It was because I wanted to reconnect to a certain place within myself. 13th-century Persian poet, Rumi, had called that place the sanctuary. I called it my haven, my sacred inner home—that space of peace and beauty where I could feel my soul. "You have to believe a little," I said. "That's what makes you feel alive. The light of faith, of magic—of love—nudges the part of you that gets excited about life and living and that makes the difference between living and existing."

Later that night, I sat with Mark in a warm bubble bath surrounded by the multitude of candles he lit before I got home. I leaned against his chest. He put his arms around me and asked if I remembered the very first time we met. "Yes," I replied with a chuckle, recalling it quite well. "You wanted me to leave."

He kissed the back of my head and then tightened his arms around my waist. Some of the tiny bath bubbles popped when he moved, and I didn't know whether it was the sound they made or the way I responded to his question that made him laugh. "I cut our conversation short for a reason," he said. "This may sound rather strange to you. However, Betsey, from the very first time I saw you on TV, I hoped we would meet. In fact, I was sure we would, especially since I was working with your brother. I guess, like many writers, sometimes I live a little too much in my head, because that day I felt devastated. Oh Betsey, when I heard you got engaged, I was almost sick."

I shifted over to look at him. He surprised me more and more. "I'm sorry to have misjudged you," I said.

"What were you going to tell me that day? You wanted to tell me something before I left."

"Yes." He sighed. I was going to ask you if you were sure Daniel was the one. I don't know. I can't explain it. I know it sounds crazy." He then paused and pointed to the window. The bathroom window was open only a tiny crack, but through it, we could hear the winter wind rattling among branches. "Listen," Mark whispered, mesmerized by the sound. "Listen," he repeated, "just for a minute. Have you ever paid attention to the wind? When I was a child my mother held down two jobs. Life wasn't easy, and to the naked eye, it wasn't always very pretty. We lived in a poor rundown section of town where litter was everywhere and especially on one particular street that was on my way to school. I hated that street. I hated it so much. It was depressing—hopeless really—until the day something magical occurred. I was walking home from school. I was nine then. Spring had arrived with a sunless sky. It looked like rain was about to pour down when, all of a sudden, this beautiful warm wind lifted bags and papers from the ground, making garbage dance off the asphalt. The wind was incredibly soothing; it also made everyone kind of look at each other in awe. I, along with the other people, men and women who lived on that street, who normally seemed either desperate or depressed, started to smile. It was a miracle. Or at least that was how it had felt to me. Just like that, we all momentarily connected. Gautama Buddha said, *'If you are quiet enough, you will hear the flow of the universe. You will feel its rhythm.'* And I did. I felt it for the first time that afternoon. Buddha also said that if we go with the universe's flow, match our hearts to it, happiness will be ours. Again, the Buddha was right, because since then, I have paid attention. Since then, I have always paid attention. And I am happy! I am so happy. I have never been happier in my life."

I almost cried when he said that. "Mark—"

"You know what else?" He smiled. "The wind carries our messages of love. It blows through the mountains of our hearts and calls to us again and again. If I die before you, which selfishly I hope I do, you will still be able to feel me. My essence will be in the wind that gently blows toward you. True love goes beyond time and space. No matter the circumstances, we will always be able to feel each other. Betsey, I have to tell you. I'm aware of how this might sound; however, I am not afraid to tell you.

The first time I saw you wasn't on TV. The first time I saw you was in a dream—one I had when I was ten years old. I used to sit under a big old elm tree in my neighborhood park, and one day when I was feeling lonely and a little sad, I yearned for the comfort of its broad spreading branches and for the soothing touch of the summer wind. My mother was working the night shift, as she often did. Really, I shouldn't have been out. This was something she was always quite strict about. However, on that particular day, I broke the rule. On that day, or rather, that evening, I went outside, sat for a while, and listened to the leaves rustle and sway. The sun had just begun to set. It was a glorious sunset that swept me into the sweetest sleep, not that I was out for very long, mind you. It seemed I slept only long enough to dream of this beautiful young girl who stood a few feet away and looked at me with a smile that was as big and as lovely as her eyes. She then began to approach me, walking toward me, slowly, very slowly—almost like she didn't want to scare me—and as soon as she got close enough, she kissed me. She kissed me on the forehead like you did on the night we first made love. Betsey, her lips were like yours and she looked like you. She felt like you. Her vibe was you. Her vibe was exactly yours."

Chapter 6

March also came quickly that year, but instead of going out like a lamb, it announced its exit with a roar when a massive storm hit New York on a Friday. Mark arrived home early that afternoon. He wasn't worried about the snow. Rather, he complained of a headache until I offered him a massage.

After a long hot shower, he got into bed and lay on his stomach while I rubbed his shoulders. "That feels so good," he moaned. "You make me feel even more than precious."

I could tell he wasn't well. His face was pale and drawn, and a slight puffiness narrowed his normally wide green eyes. Eventually, I went to lie beside him, and he smiled at me and whispered. He said, "The coin really doesn't matter."

"Coin?" I questioned. "What coin?"

"The one I almost threw into the fountain outside my office building two years ago. Betsey, you know, a couple of years ago, my life wasn't going very well. I almost lost everything—my magazine, my reputation, my health—and worse than anything, I almost lost my spirit. It was a dark time. I was scared—very scared. People were threatening me. I was receiving menacing letters, e-mails, and comments on my blog. At first they were saying I was crazy. Then they started calling me a pervert. You name it, I got it, and it got even worse when the character attacks turned into a physical assault that made me sick. From the moment I hit the ground that night, I was dizzy and nauseous, and it went on for weeks."

He looked like he was about to cry. He was fragile that night, physically and emotionally, which was something I wasn't used to. "They really hurt me, Betsey—physically

Chapter 6

and morally. They wanted to take away my life, because they didn't like my magazine. That person who attacked me threw me down as if I were nothing. I was lying on the ground, unable to move, and I pleaded with him to leave me alone—I begged him. You know, if it wouldn't have been for Gordo coming out of the building when he did...if it wouldn't have been for him..." His voice hoarsened. He started to shake. And suddenly, a part of me began to feel uneasy. There was still this part of me that was, in a way, constricted and uncomfortable with vulnerability. For a moment, I wanted to escape. I wanted to leave him be, but then just as suddenly, something else took over. Something stronger than "that part of me" implored me to stay and to hold him tightly in my arms, so tightly that I could barely distinguish his heartbeat from mine.

"I'm sorry, honey," he sighed. "I didn't mean to spill on you. What I wanted to tell you is that two years ago, I felt like I was going to die, and then all of a sudden, I saw you and—"

"You saw me, when?"

"When you were standing outside Gordo's on a blustery rainy night, looking up to me, not quite knowing what to do. So many times I've wanted to tell you that I saw you that night. There was a power outage, and I had gone to blow out the candle by the window when something told me to look outside. I'm sorry, I didn't call out to you. I wanted to with all my heart, but everything was spinning around me, and I couldn't manage the window's lock."

I almost couldn't believe it. A shiver ran down my spine.

"The second I saw you," he said, "I knew, I just knew I was going to be all right. You're my hero."

His gaze, through eyes that had been brimming with tears, was so soft and sweet, and I hugged him again, burying my face in his hair that smelled of shampoo. "You smell like heaven." I smiled. "I love you."

Like his mother had said, life hadn't been easy for Mark. His very first breaths were a fight. Growing up was another fight against loneliness and poverty. And then, once he prevailed and became successful, people tried to destroy him. They tried to take it away. I couldn't stop thinking of how scared he said he had been and how much he must have suffered alone.

Chapter 6

Exhausted, he soon fell asleep, and I settled into the living room, trying to distract myself with schoolwork. I tried, but couldn't focus. I couldn't write a word until turning to my journal. I figured that might help. Sometimes a little journaling got me going. This was one of those times. Before I knew it, I was writing up a storm, describing an afternoon where I had found Mark sleeping on the daybed. It was really just a big padded sill, part of the bay window next to our fireplace; however, it was quite cozy. Mark loved to lie on its large comfortable cushions. Secretly, I did too. Every afternoon, after school, he would still be at work, and I'd immerse myself in those pillows that smelled like his shampoo. I always looked forward to it, but never as much as I did that day. That particular day, I couldn't wait. All the way home, I dreamed of snuggling into our daybed. I even started walking faster to get there. Faster and faster I strode, until finally, I opened the door and found that Mark had beaten me to it.

I wrote about how he slept that day on that large padded sill—how he looked and how I felt when I saw him. Whether sleeping or awake, he was always so comfortable. His essence, his body, and his mind were one, which was why he was never afraid to feel.

He was never afraid to feel emotions that ran infi-nitely deep, nor was he fearful to express them.

Tears unexpectedly fell to my paper, smudging some of the ink. Both Mark and Max ran into the room, but I only realized how hard I was crying when I couldn't catch my breath. The emotion, bursting from my heart, was so strong; it felt as if everyone I had ever loved in my life, starting with my grandmother, was bringing me to my knees.

"Oh, honey," Mark moaned, pressing me to his chest. His heart was racing. I was scaring him. I knew it. I could feel it. But I also couldn't help it. It was like something inside me had broken and left my heart completely exposed.

"Betsey, come," he said, leading me by the hand to the daybed. "Honey," he whispered, "look outside." The storm was well underway. Blankets of falling snow glistened in the light. Shadows danced. So much beauty covered the earth. And I began to calm down. "Honey," Mark whispered again. "Do you know what I think?"

"What?" I sighed.

Chapter 6

"That the snow loves the trees as much as I love you. This is why it touches them so gently. It would never want to hurt them, and I would never do or say anything to hurt you. You can tell me anything, and I promise I won't get angry or—"

"Hold me," I said. "Mark, please, hold me again."

"Betsey, I'm worried."

"No, love, don't. There is nothing for you to worry about."

His eyes were still puffy, the tip of his nose red, and his long hair characteristically disheveled, but to me he was beautiful, the most beautiful man in the world. I pushed his hair behind his ears and caressed his face with my fingers. "You know," I said, "I never used to sit here. Now, I sit on this sill every afternoon because the pillows smell like you, because they smell like your shampoo. I can't be without you, and it seems I never am. You are with me everywhere I go. I have never felt like this before. I didn't believe I could. I'd lost faith in myself that way."

"Betsey—"

"No, please, let me finish. You don't understand, or maybe you do. I don't know…"

He smiled. "I think I do."

"I can feel it now!" I exclaimed. I can FEEL that indomitable power we call true love. It's not projection, dependency, or lust. It is LOVE, and it's made me realize that I have something to give. I never thought of myself as having much to offer another person. Perhaps that was why I didn't wanted to have children until now. When I was younger, I used to think I wasn't far enough along in life to want a family. Then, as the years went by, I started to consider that there could be something wrong with me—that I was missing the nurturing gene."

Mark put his hand to his head, rubbed his temples, and slightly raised his voice. "Betsey," he said, "I love *you*. Do you understand? I love you so much that sometimes I can't breathe. Yesterday morning I woke up, and the way you were looking at me, the way that made me feel…the way you made me feel earlier when you rubbed my back…the way you're making me feel right now…You're not missing the nurturing gene. You're not missing anything."

"I know...I know that now. As ridiculous as this may sound, I've returned to myself and have never felt so happy, nor have I felt so much love and compassion in my life. You called me your hero, but in the end, it was you who helped to rescue me."

His top lip started to quiver, but his voice remained strong. "Betsey, I want to marry you," he said. "I want to marry you and have two, four, five children. Is that too many?"

"No." I smiled, deliriously happy. "That sounds absolutely right!"

Two months later, spring had arrived. Birds were singing, and so was I, as I planned our wedding. Everybody was excited about it—everyone, including my brother whose eyes had more than just a twinkle when he came over for coffee one morning after Mark had left for work.

"Betsey," he said. "You look beautiful!"

"Beautiful," I said, "is exactly how I feel."

"I know." He smiled. "It shows. And it shows on Mark too. He's in heaven."

"He is heaven!" I exclaimed.

John smiled again. "I guess little brother knows a thing or two," he said. "But then, so does big sister…"

"Really?" I said before sitting down. "Tell me, what do you mean?"

"Well," he sighed, "I've found heaven too."

"You did? In what way?"

"In the way that I did what you suggested. I connected with Gigi through meditation. Or, at least, that was what it felt like."

"John—"

"I don't know. Maybe I'm crazy, or lonely, or both; but in my last meditation, I experienced something that gave me a very deep sense of peace."

"Tell me," I said. "Tell me everything."

"All right," he replied, "here goes! That meditation—that prolonged meditation—resulted in a
vision through which I saw myself in a little church,
standing with Gigi at the altar. She was wearing a
white satin dress, holding a white rose bouquet, and
I understood we were being married on a spiritual
plane. We exchanged vows and rings, and she kissed
me. Boy did she kiss me! Almost instantly, I felt a wave
of peace wash through my mind, and at that moment,
I realized that the purpose of my meeting and falling in love with her was about cementing my belief in
something greater than what my eyes can see. Also,
after we kissed, Gigi pointed to another woman who
was standing a few feet away from her and carrying a
more colorful bouquet. This signified something to
me, as well. It implied moving forward, which I am
now ready to do."

So many years earlier, my grandmother told us true
love brings great peace. There was no doubt in my
mind about the reality of John's experience. The more
love touched my soul, the more I could see beyond
the limits. There are infinite channels through which
love can appear to us, because each soul—whether it
be on earth or in heaven—is a highly creative power.
Love is there for the finding in the ordinary and the

unexpected if we open our hearts wide enough. If we open our hearts wide enough to pray, to listen, and to heal, love will find us even when we're sitting very still.

46053575R00059

Made in the USA
Lexington, KY
22 October 2015